THE FACE OF JESUS

POPE BENEDICT XVI

SPIRITUAL THOUGHTS SERIES

"Your face, LORD, do I seek!"
Psalm 27:8

Introduction by Lucio Coco

United States Conference of Catholic Bishops
Washington, DC

First Printing, January 2012
ISBN 978-1-60137-195-9

CONTENTS

elping others to see the true Face of God is the first form of love.

Benedict XVI

INTRODUCTION

his volume of the series of the *Spiritual Thoughts* of Pope Benedict XVI is a collection of some of the Holy Father's reflections on the Face of Christ, on Jesus as the Face of God, on the Face of the Passion and on the reflection that this face produces in our lives, on how our decisions can make our own image conform more and more to the divine features, so that our Christian identity can become deeper and more fully formed.

In today's reality, so overloaded with images, the Face of Christ that Pope Benedict offers and indicates continually for our contemplation expresses an essential figure to the construction of which we must contribute our entire lives. Over and over again, he echoes the invitation of the Psalmist to "constantly seek his face" (Ps 105:4) and the commentary of St. Augustine that emphasizes that this search is inexhaustible and endures for all eternity: in fact, the more we enter into the splendor of this face, "the greater will be our discoveries and the more beautiful it will be to travel on and know that our seeking has no end, hence, finding has no end and is thus eternity—the joy of seeking and at the same time of finding" (Address at the 20th World Youth Day, August 21, 2005).

In this journey of exploration and seeking, the other important and decisive relationship that Pope Benedict highlights is the one through which Jesus manifests the Face of the Father. He is the "revelation," and his Face shows us who the Father is: "God is not an unknown Person, a hypothesis perhaps of the very beginning of the cosmos.

God is flesh and blood. He is one of us. We know him by his Face, by his Name. He is Jesus Christ" (Address to Parish Priests and the Clergy of the Diocese of Rome, February 7, 2008). The contours of this face provide a glimpse of the features of the face of God, they reveal his merciful face, "the Face of pardon and love, the Face of the encounter with us" (Lenten Meeting with the Clergy of Rome, February 22, 2007). The God of Revelation is not, therefore, just any sort of God, cold and distant like the god of the philosophers, but a God who out of love stoops down to humanity, allowing himself to be wounded in order to heal its wounds. He is a God who has suffered for us, and who with his Passion and through his disfigured face, so cruelly shown to us in the Stations of the Cross, continues to reflect for us the "Face of the One who transforms the world in the manner of the grain of wheat that fell into the earth" (Meeting with the Diocesan Clergy of Aosta, July 25, 2005).

"We want to see Jesus," said some of the Greeks who had gone to Jerusalem for the Passover (cf. Jn 12:20-22). In the request of these men, the Holy Father sees "the thirst to see and to know Christ which is in every person's heart" (Homily for the Fifth Sunday of Lent, March 29, 2009). And the response that Jesus gave and that made him known to the men was that of losing oneself for the sake of giving oneself: "Amen, amen, I say to you, unless a grain of wheat falls to the ground and dies, it remains just a grain of wheat; but if it dies, it produces much fruit. Whoever loves his life loses it, and whoever hates his life in this world will preserve it for eternal life" (Jn 12:24-25).

The Gospel does not say whether these anonymous pilgrims listened to this teaching, or instead returned to Greece without succeeding in "seeing Jesus"; that is, whether they were able to impress his face upon themselves, to stamp it on their hearts in terms of openness, of capacity for service, of self-giving, of losing oneself for the sake of finding oneself as is written of the grain of wheat that must die in order to bear much fruit.

The image of the cross is therefore inscribed on the face of Christ as the most certain sign of the true transformation of the human person, of becoming like him in no other feature if not that of the capacity to suffer and to love, because, as Pope Benedict reminds us, there is no other way to experience the joy and the true fecundity of love than "the way of giving oneself, of self-giving, of losing oneself in order to find oneself" (Homily for the Fifth Sunday of Lent, March 29, 2009).

Lucio Coco

THE FACE OF JESUS

1. Longing

"Your Face, O Lord, I seek": seeking the Face of Jesus must be the longing of all of us Christians; indeed, we are "the generation" which seeks his Face in our day, the Face of the "God of Jacob." If we persevere in our quest for the Face of the Lord, at the end of our earthly pilgrimage, he, Jesus, will be our eternal joy, our reward and glory for ever: "*Sis Jesu nostrum gaudium, qui es futurus praemium: sit nostra in te gloria, per cuncta semper saecula.*"

> *Address during a pilgrimage to the Shrine of the*
> *Holy Face in Manoppello, Italy*
> *September 1, 2006*

I. "CONSTANTLY SEEK HIS FACE"

2. *Invitation*

St. Augustine . . . has some marvelous thoughts about the invitation found in Psalm 105[104]: "*Quaerite faciem eius semper*—constantly seek his face" (v. 3).

He points out that this invitation is not only valid for this life but also for eternity. The discovery of "God's Face" is never ending. The further we penetrate into the splendor of divine love, the more beautiful it is to pursue our search, so that "*amore crescente inquisitio crescat inventi*—the greater love grows, the further we will seek the One who has been found" (*Enarr. in Ps* 105[104]: 3; *CCL* 40, 1537).

This is the experience to which, deep down, we too aspire.

Angelus
August 28, 2005

3. *Searching*

Today, many people are searching. We too are searching. Basically, in a different dialectic, both these things must always exist within us. We must respect each one's own search. We must sustain it and make them feel that faith is not merely a dogmatism complete in itself that puts an end to seeking, that extinguishes man's great thirst, but that it directs the great pilgrimage towards the infinite; we, as believers, are always simultaneously seekers and finders.

In his Commentary on the Psalms, St. Augustine interprets so splendidly the expression "*Quaerite faciem eius semper*," "constantly seek his face," that ever since my student days his words have lived on in my heart. This is not only true for this life, but for eternity; his face will be one to ceaselessly rediscover. The more deeply we penetrate the splendor of divine love, the greater will be our discoveries and the more beautiful it will be to travel on and know that our seeking has no end, hence, finding has no end and is thus eternity—the joy of seeking and at the same time of finding.

We must support people in their search as fellow-seekers, and at the same time we must also give them the certainty that God has found us and, consequently, that we can find him.

Address to German Bishops during an apostolic journey to Cologne August 21, 2005

4. *On the way*

Faith in Christ brought all Augustine's seeking to fulfillment, but fulfillment in the sense that he always remained on the way. Indeed, he tells us: even in eternity our seeking will not be completed, it will be an eternal adventure, the discovery of new greatness, new beauty.

He interpreted the words of the Psalm, "Seek his face continually," and said: this is true for eternity; and the beauty of eternity is that it is not a static reality but immense progress in the immense beauty of God.

Thus, he could discover God as the founding reason, but also as love which embraces us, guides us and gives meaning to history and to our personal life.

Address to the representatives of the World of Culture
April 22, 2007

5. *Conversions*

Just as prior to his baptism Augustine's life was a journey of conversion, after it too, although differently, his life continued to be a journey of conversion—until his last illness, when he had the penitential Psalms hung on the walls so that he might have them always before his eyes, and when he excluded himself from receiving the Eucharist in order to go back once again over the path of his repentance and receive salvation from Christ's hands as a gift of God's mercy.

Thus, we can rightly speak of Augustine's "conversions," which actually consisted of one important conversion in his quest for the Face of Christ and then in the journeying on with him.

Homily of the Third Sunday of Easter
April 22, 2007

6. *To know him*

Those who ascend it and truly desire to reach the heights, to arrive at the true summit, must be people who question themselves about God. They must be people who scan their surroundings seeking God, seeking his Face. . . . How important precisely this is today: not merely to let oneself be taken here and there in life; not to be satisfied with what everyone else thinks and says and does. To probe God and to seek God. Not letting the question about God dissolve in our souls; desiring what is greater, desiring to know him—his Face.

Homily at the 22nd World Youth Day
April 1, 2007

7. *To young people*

Dear friends, like the young St. Augustine, with all his problems on his difficult path, each one of you, every creature, hears the symbolic call from above; every beautiful creature is attracted back to the beauty of the Creator, who is effectively concentrated in the Face of Jesus Christ. When the soul experiences this, it exclaims, "Late have I loved you, o beauty ever ancient ever new, late have I loved you!" (*Conf.* X, 27.38). May each one of you rediscover God as the sense and foundation of every creature, light of truth, flame of charity, bond of unity.

Address to the young people of Sardinia
September 7, 2008

8. *Desire*

May [the Lord] "make his face to shine" upon us, "and be gracious" to us (cf. Nm 6:24-7) and bless us. We may be certain of it: if we never tire of seeking his Face, if we never give in to the temptation of discouragement and doubt, if also among the many difficulties we encounter we always remain anchored to him, we will experience the power of his love and his mercy.

> *Homily on the Solemnity of Mary, Mother of God,*
> *and the 41st World Day of Peace*
> *January 1, 2008*

II. JESUS, THE FACE OF GOD

The infinite beauty of God . . . shines on Christ's Face.

—HOMILY AT PAUL VI SQUARE IN BRESCIA, ITALY
NOVEMBER 8, 2009

9. *Name and face*

For Christians, truth has a name: God. And goodness has a face: Jesus Christ.

Address at the Presidential Palace of Prague
September 26, 2009

10. *Revelation*

Jesus' voice reveal[s] to us the Face of his Father and our Father. Basically, this was the reason he came into the world: to speak to us of the Father; to make him known to us, his lost children, and to revive in our hearts the joy of belonging to him, the hope of being forgiven and restored to our full dignity, the desire to dwell for ever in his house which is also our house.

Angelus
September 16, 2007

11. *In relationship*

God is not an unknown Person, a hypothesis perhaps of the very beginning of the cosmos. God is flesh and blood. He is one of us. We know him by his Face, by his Name. He is Jesus Christ who speaks to us in the Gospel. He is both man and God. And being God, he chose man to enable us to choose God. Thus, we must enter into the knowledge of Jesus and then friendship with him in order to walk with him.

Address to the priests and the clergy
of the Diocese of Rome
February 7, 2008

12. *Discovery*

Only if we manage to grasp that Jesus is not a great prophet or a world religious figure but that he is the Face of God, that he is God, have we discovered Christ's greatness and found out who God is. God is not only a distant shadow, the "primary Cause," but he has a Face. His is the Face of mercy, the Face of pardon and love, the Face of the encounter with us. As a result, these two topics penetrate each other and must always go together.

Address to the clergy of Rome
February 22, 2007

13. *Transformation*

The world cannot live without God, the God of Revelation—and not just any God: we see how dangerous a cruel

God, an untrue God can be—the God who showed us his Face in Jesus Christ. This Face of the One who suffered for us, this loving Face of the One who transforms the world in the manner of the grain of wheat that fell into the earth.

Address to the diocesan clergy of Aosta
July 25, 2005

14. *Certainty*

Therefore, we ourselves have this very deep certainty that Christ is the answer and that without the concrete God, the God with the Face of Christ, the world destroys itself; and there is growing evidence that a closed rationalism, which thinks that human beings can rebuild the world better on their own, is not true. On the contrary, without the restraint of the true God, human beings destroy themselves. We see this with our own eyes.

Address to the diocesan clergy of Aosta
July 25, 2005

15. *Simplicity*

In the end, faith is simple and rich: we believe that God exists, that God counts; but which God? A God with a face, a human face, a God who reconciles, who overcomes hatred and gives us the power of peace that no one else can give us. We must make people understand that Christianity is actually very simple and consequently very rich.

Address to the diocesan clergy of Aosta
July 25, 2005

16. *Along the right path*

So it is important to discover the true face of God. The Magi from the East found it when they knelt down before the Child of Bethlehem. "Anyone who has seen me has seen the Father," said Jesus to Philip (Jn 14:9). In Jesus Christ, who allowed his heart to be pierced for us, the true face of God is seen. We will follow him together with the great multitude of those who went before us. Then we will be traveling along the right path.

Address on the occasion of the 20th World Youth Day
August 20, 2005

17. *Novelty*

A novelty appears that surpasses all human research, the novelty that only God himself can reveal to us: the novelty of a love that moved God to take on a human face, even to take on flesh and blood, the entire human being.

The *eros* of God is not only a primordial cosmic power; it is love that created man and that bows down over him, as the Good Samaritan bent down to the wounded and robbed man, lying on the side of the road that went down from Jerusalem to Jericho.

Address to the participants at the meeting promoted by
the Pontifical Council "Cor Unum"
January 23, 2006

18. *Paradox*

To express ourselves in accordance with the paradox of the Incarnation we can certainly say that God gave himself a human face, the Face of Jesus, and consequently, from now on, if we truly want to know the Face of God, all we have to do is to contemplate the Face of Jesus! In his Face we truly see who God is and what he looks like!

General Audience
September 6, 2006

19. *Nearness*

If we now use the word "God," it is no longer a reality known only from afar. We know the Face of God: it is that of the Son, who came to bring the heavenly realities closer to us and to the earth.

General Audience
January 3, 2007

20. *Truth*

The truth revealed, when "the time had fully come" (Gal 4:4), assumed the Face of a person, Jesus of Nazareth, who brought the ultimate and definitive answer to the question of human meaning. The truth of Christ, since it affects every person in search of joy, happiness and meaning, far exceeds any other truth that reason can discover. It surrounds mystery, so that *fides* and *ratio* might find the real possibility of a common path.

Address on the 10th anniversary of the publication of Fides et Ratio
October 16, 2008

21. *Knowledge*

Knowledge can never be limited to the purely intellectual realm; it also includes a renewed ability to look at things in a way free of prejudices and preconceptions, and to allow ourselves to be "amazed" by reality, whose truth can be discovered by uniting understanding with love. Only the God who has a human face, revealed in Jesus Christ, can prevent us from truncating reality at the very moment when it demands ever new and more complex levels of understanding.

Address to the participants in the first
European Meeting of University Lecturers
June 23, 2007

22. *Unity*

The *unity* of men and women in their multiplicity has become possible because God, this one God of heaven and earth, has shown himself to us; because the essential truth about our lives, our "where from?" and "where to?" became visible when he revealed himself to us and enabled us to see his face, himself, in Jesus Christ. This truth about the essence of our being, living and dying, a truth that God made visible, unites us and makes us brothers and sisters. *Catholicity* and *unity* go hand in hand. And *unity* has a content: the faith that the Apostles passed on to us in Christ's name.

Homily on the Solemnity of Ss. Peter and Paul
June 29, 2005

23. *Learning*

In the story of Jesus we learn . . . the Face of God, we learn what God is like. It is important to know Jesus deeply, personally. That way he enters into our life and, through our life, enters into the world.

Dialogue with the children of the
Pontifical Society of the Holy Childhood
May 30, 2009

24. *Blessing*

Jesus is the Face of God, he is the blessing for every person and for all peoples, he is peace for the world.

Angelus
January 1, 2010

III. THE FACE OF THE PASSION

25. *Manifestation*

God revealed himself in the humility of the "human form," in the "form of a slave," indeed, of one who died on a cross (cf. Phil 2:6-8). This is the Christian paradox.

Indeed, this very concealment constitutes the most eloquent "manifestation" of God. The humility, poverty, even the ignominy of the Passion enable us to know what God is truly like. The Face of the Son faithfully reveals that of the Father.

Homily on the Solemnity of the Epiphany
January 6, 2006

26. *Kenosis*

God does not leave us groping in the dark. He has shown himself to us as a man. In his greatness he has let himself become small. "Whoever has seen me has seen the Father," Jesus says (Jn 14:9). God has taken on a human face. He has loved us even to the point of letting himself be nailed to the Cross for our sake, in order to bring the sufferings of mankind to the very heart of God.

Homily at Islinger Feld, Regensburg
September 12, 2006

27. *Light*

We see more and more clearly that on our own we cannot foster justice and peace unless the light of a God who shows us his Face is revealed to us, a God who appears to us in the manger of Bethlehem, who appears to us on the Cross.

Homily on the Solemnity of the Epiphany
January 6, 2007

28. *Questions*

What have we done with the revelation of the Face of God in Christ, with the revelation of God's love that conquers hate? Many, in our age as well, do not know God and cannot find him in the crucified Christ. Many are in search of a love or a liberty that excludes God. Many believe they have no need of God. Dear friends: After having lived together Jesus' Passion, let us this evening allow his sacrifice on the Cross to question us. Let us permit him to put our human certainties in crisis. Let us open our hearts to him. Jesus is the truth that makes us free to love.

Address on Good Friday
March 21, 2008

29. *Need*

At this very moment—the moment of a widespread abuse of God's Name—we need God who triumphs on the Cross, who does not conquer with violence but with his love. At this very moment we need the Face of Christ in order to know the true Face of God and thus bring reconciliation and light to this world.

Address at the Parish of Rhêmes-Saint Georges
July 23, 2006

30. *Image*

"To gaze upon Christ": let us look briefly now at the Crucified One above the high altar. God saved the world not by the sword, but by the Cross. In dying, Jesus extends his arms. This, in the first place, is the posture of the Passion, in which he lets himself be nailed to the Cross for us, in order to give us his life. Yet outstretched arms are also the posture of one who prays, the stance assumed by the priest when he extends his arms in prayer: Jesus transformed the Passion, his suffering and his death, into prayer, and in this way he transformed it into an act of love for God and for humanity. That, finally, is why the outstretched arms of the Crucified One are also a gesture of embracing, by which he draws us to himself, wishing to enfold us in his loving hands. In this way he is an image of the living God, he is God himself, and we may entrust ourselves to him.

Homily in front of the Basilica of Mariazell
September 8, 2007

31. *Extraordinary adventure*

To see God, to orient oneself to God, know God, know God's will, enter into the will that is, into the love of God is to enter ever more into the space of truth. And this journey of coming to know God, of loving relationship with God, is the extraordinary adventure of our Christian life; for in Christ we know the face of God, the face of God that loves us even unto the Cross, unto the gift of himself.

Address on the annual Feast of Our Lady of Trust
February 20, 2009

32. Response

It seems to me that if we look at the panorama of the world situation today, one can understand—I would say even humanly, almost without the need of having recourse to faith—that the God who has taken on a human face, the God who has become incarnate, whose name is Jesus Christ and who has suffered for us, this God is needed by all and is the only response to all the challenges of this time.

Address to the members of the Italian Episcopal
Conference at the 57th General Assembly
May 24, 2007

33. God-with-us

If we do not know God in and with Christ, all of reality is transformed into an indecipherable enigma; there is no way, and without a way, there is neither life nor truth.

God is the foundational reality, not a God who is merely imagined or hypothetical, but God with a human face; he is God-with-us, the God who loves even to the Cross.

Address to the bishops of Latin America
and the Caribbean
May 13, 2007

34. *Requirement*

Is there still a need for God? Is it still reasonable to believe in God? Is Christ merely a figure in the history of religion or is he truly the Face of God that we all need? Can we live to the full without knowing Christ?

It is necessary to understand that building life and the future also requires patience and suffering. Nor can the Cross be lacking.

Address to the diocesan clergy of Aosta
July 25, 2005

35. *Beatitude*

Jesus, with his death on the Cross and his Resurrection, has revealed his Face to us, the face of a God so great in love as to communicate to us an uncrushable hope that not even death can break, because the life of the one who entrusts himself to this Father opens itself to the prospect of eternal beatitude.

Angelus
December 2, 2007

36. *True face*

From the outset the disciples recognized the Risen Jesus as the One who is our brother in humanity but is also one with God; the One who, with his coming into the world and throughout his life, in his death and in his Resurrection, brought us God and in a new and unique way made God present in the world: the One, therefore, who gives meaning and hope to our life; in fact, it is in him that we encounter the true Face of God, that we find what we really need in order to live.

Address at the convention of the Diocese of Rome
June 11, 2007

37. *Transfiguration*

On the transfigured face of Jesus a ray of light which he held within shines forth. This same light was to shine on Christ's face on the day of the Resurrection. In this sense, the Transfiguration appears as a foretaste of the Paschal Mystery.

Angelus
August 6, 2006

38. *Gaze*

The Holy Face of Jesus [is] that Face which "some Greeks," of which the Gospel speaks, wished to see; that Face which in the coming days of the Passion we shall contemplate disfigured by human sins, indifference and ingratitude; that Face, radiant with light and dazzling with glory that will shine out at dawn on Easter Day. Let us keep our hearts and minds fixed on the Face of Christ.

Homily on the Fifth Sunday of Lent
March 29, 2009

39. *Reflection*

Let us pause this evening to contemplate his disfigured face: it is the face of the Man of sorrows, who took upon himself the burden of all our mortal anguish. His face is reflected in that of every person who is humiliated and offended, sick and suffering, alone, abandoned and despised. Pouring out his blood, he has rescued us from the slavery of death, he has broken the solitude of our tears, he has entered into our every grief and our every anxiety.

Address on Good Friday
April 10, 2009

IV. MARY, MOTHER OF THE HOLY FACE

40. *Features*

[In the face of] Our Lady . . .—more than in any other creature—we can recognize the features of the Incarnate Word.

*Address during a pilgrimage to the Shrine of the Holy
Face in Manoppello, Italy
September 1, 2006*

41. *Guide*

In contemplating the face of Christ, and in Christ, the face
of the Father, Mary Most Holy precedes, sustains and
accompanies us.

*Address to the Italian Bishops' Conference
May 30, 2005*

42. *Preeminence*

God's Face took on a human face, letting itself be seen and
recognized in the Son of the Virgin Mary, who for this reason we venerate with the loftiest title of "Mother of God."
She, who had preserved in her heart the secret of the divine

motherhood, was the first to see the face of God made man in the small fruit of her womb.

Homily on the Solemnity of Mary, Mother of God, and
the 43rd World Day of Peace
January 1, 2010

43. *By the hand*

It is first of all necessary to let the Blessed Virgin take one by the hand to contemplate the Face of Christ: a joyful, luminous, sorrowful and glorious Face. Those who, like Mary and with her, cherish and ponder the mysteries of Jesus assiduously, increasingly assimilate his sentiments and are conformed to him.

Meditation during a pastoral visit to the Pontifical Shrine
of Pompeii
October 19, 2008

44. *Prayer*

"To gaze upon Christ" is the motto of this day. For one who is searching, this summons repeatedly turns into a spontaneous plea, a plea addressed especially to Mary, who has given us Christ as her Son: "Show us Jesus!" Let us make this prayer today with our whole heart; let us make this prayer above and beyond the present moment, as we inwardly seek the Face of the Redeemer. "Show us Jesus!," Mary.

Homily in front of the Basilica of Mariazell
September 8, 2007

45. *The heart of peace*

Let us ask Mary, Mother of God, to help us to welcome her Son and, in him, true peace. Let us ask her to sharpen our perception so that we may recognize in the face of every human person, the Face of Christ, the heart of peace!

Homily on the Solemnity of Mary, Mother of God, and
the 40th World Day of Peace
January 1, 2007

V. THE CHURCH, THE FACE OF CHRIST

46. *Responsibility*

[The Church] is not made of material stones but of living stones, of baptized people who feel the full responsibility of the faith for others, the full joy of being baptized and knowing God in the face of Jesus.

Address to the pastoral workers of the Roman Parish of
"Dio Padre Misericordiso"
March 26, 2006

47. *Contemplation*

Taking up the teaching of John Paul II in *Novo Millennio Ineunte,* you rightly base everything on contemplation of Jesus Christ, and in him, of the true face of God the Father and the living, daily relationship with him.

Here, in fact, lies the heart and the secret energy of the Church, the source of our apostolate's effectiveness. Especially in the mystery of the Eucharist, we ourselves, our priests and all our faithful can live to the full this relationship with Christ: here he becomes tangible among us, he gives himself ever anew, he becomes ours, so that we may become his and learn his love.

Address to the Italian Bishops' Conference
May 30, 2005

48. *Presence*

Here in the Sacred Host [Jesus] is present before us and in our midst. As at that time, so now he is mysteriously veiled in a sacred silence; as at that time, it is here that the true face of God is revealed. For us he became a grain of wheat that falls on the ground and dies and bears fruit until the end of the world (cf. Jn 12:24).

He is present . . . [and] he invites us to that inner pilgrimage which is called adoration. Let us set off on this pilgrimage of the spirit and let us ask him to be our guide.

Address during the youth vigil at the
20th World Youth Day
August 20, 2005

49. *Time*

The time of the Church, the time of the Spirit: the Spirit is the Teacher who trains *disciples:* he teaches them to love Jesus; he trains them to hear his word and to contemplate his countenance; he conforms them to Christ's sacred humanity, a humanity which is poor in spirit, afflicted, meek, hungry for justice, merciful, pure in heart, peacemaking, persecuted for justice's sake (cf. Mt 5:3-10).

Homily in front of the Shrine of Aparecida
May 13, 2007

50. *Priests* (1)

Dear priests, we can never sufficiently emphasize how fundamental and crucial our personal response to the call to holiness is. It is not only the condition for our personal apostolate to be fruitful but also, and more generally, for the face of the Church to reflect the light of Christ (cf. *Lumen Gentium,* no. 1), thereby inducing people to recognize and adore the Lord.

We must first inwardly accept the Apostle Paul's plea that we let ourselves be reconciled to God (cf. 2 Cor 5:20), asking the Lord with a sincere heart and courageous determination to take away from us all that separates us from God and is contrary to the mission we have received. The Lord is merciful, we are certain, and will answer our prayer.

Address to the clergy of Rome
May 13, 2005

51. *Priests* (2)

Dear [priests], the more you seek the Face of Christ, so much better can you serve the Church and the Christian and non-Christian people whom you will meet on your path.

Address to superiors and students of the Pontifical
Ecclesiastical Academy
June 2, 2007

52. *Evangelizing*

The act of evangelization consists precisely in the fact that the distant God draws near, that he is no longer far away, but is close to us, that this "known and unknown" figure now makes himself truly known, shows his Face, reveals himself: the veil covering his Face disappears and he shows his true Face. And so, since God himself is now near us, we can know him, he shows us his Face and enters our world. There is no longer any need to make do with those other powers, because he is the true power, the Omnipotent.

Homily during the celebration of Vespers
at the Cathedral of Aosta
July 24, 2009

53. *Apostles*

"No one knows the Father except the Son" (Mt 11:27). Jesus himself experienced the rejection of God by the world, the misunderstanding, the indifference, the disfiguration of the Face of God. And Jesus passed the "witness" on to the disciples: "I made known to them your name," he further confides in the prayer to the Father, "and I will make it known, that the love with which you have loved me may be in them, and I in them" (Jn 17:26). Therefore the disciple and especially the apostle experiences the same joy that Jesus did, in knowing the name and the Face of the Father; and also shares his suffering, seeing that God is not recognized, that his love is not returned.

Homily at St. Peter's Basilica
May 3, 2009

54. *Formation*

Formation . . . has different strands which converge in the unity of the person: it includes human, spiritual and cultural dimensions. Its deepest goal is to bring the student to an intimate knowledge of the God who has revealed his face in Jesus Christ.

For this, in-depth study of Sacred Scripture is needed, and also of the faith and life of the Church in which the Scripture dwells as the Word of life. This must all be linked with the questions prompted by our reason and with the broader context of modern life.

Address to seminarians during the 20th World Youth Day
August 19, 2005

55. *Proclamation*

Ecumenical training should be intensified, starting from the foundations of the Christian faith, that is, from the proclamation of the love of God who revealed himself in the Face of Jesus Christ, and at the same time revealed man to himself and brought to light his most high calling (cf. *Gaudium et Spes,* no. 22).

Address at the Pontifical Council for
Promoting Christian Unity
November 17, 2006

56. *The mission of the Church*

The core of all cultural training, which is so necessary, must undoubtedly be faith: to know the face of God, revealed in Christ, and thus to have the fundamental point of reference for the rest of culture, which would otherwise become disoriented and disorienting. A culture without a personal knowledge of God and without a knowledge of the face of God in Christ is a culture that could be destructive, because it would have no knowledge of the necessary ethical bearings. In this regard, I think, we really have a profound cultural and human mission, which opens people to all the wealth of the culture of our time but also provides the criterion, the discernment to test what is true culture and what might become anti-culture.

Address to the parish priests and the clergy
of the Diocese of Rome
February 26, 2009

57. *Path*

The face of the Church . . . reflects Christ's light upon us and upon the whole world. . . . The Church renews the mystery for people of every generation, she shows them God's Face so that, with his Blessing, they may walk on the path of peace.

Homily on the Solemnity of Mary, Mother of God,
and the 43rd World Day of Peace
January 1, 2010

VI. THE FACE OF CHRIST REFLECTED IN OUR LIVES

58. *Choosing a relationship*

A world empty of God, a world that has forgotten God, loses life and relapses into a culture of death.

Choosing life, taking the option for life, therefore, means first and foremost choosing the option of a relationship with God. However, the question immediately arises: with which God? Here, once again, the Gospel helps us: with the God who showed us his face in Christ, the God who overcame hatred on the Cross, that is, in love to the very end. Thus, by choosing this God, we choose life.

Address to members of the Roman clergy
March 2, 2006

59. *Secret*

Even if one has all he or she wants, one can sometimes be unhappy; on the other hand, one can be deprived of everything, even freedom or health, and be in peace and joy if God is in his or her heart.

Thus, the secret is this: God must always have first place in our life. And Jesus has revealed the true face of God to us.

Address during a visit to Rome's prison for minors,
"Casal del Marmo"
March 18, 2007

60. *True life*

God . . . has shown us his face in Jesus, who suffered for us, who loved us to the point of dying, and thus overcame violence. It is necessary to make the living God present in our "own" lives first of all, the God who is not a stranger, a fictitious God, a God only thought of, but a God who has shown himself, who has shown his being and his face.

Only in this way do our lives become true, authentically human; hence, the criteria of true humanism emerge in society.

Meeting with youth in St. Peter's Square
April 6, 2006

61. *Yes*

The Christian option is basically very simple: it is the option to say "yes" to life. But this "yes" only takes place with a God who is known, with a God with a human face. It takes place by following this God in the communion of love.

Address to members of the Roman clergy
March 2, 2006

62. *In contact*

We feel how beautiful it is that he is there and that we can know him—that we know him in the face of Jesus Christ who suffered for us.

I think this is the first thing: that we ourselves enter into vital contact with God—with the Lord Jesus, the living God; that in us the organ directed to God be strengthened; that we bear within us a perception of his "exquisiteness."

Homily at Mass with the members of the
Bishops' Conference of Switzerland
November 7, 2006

63. *Communion*

In order to enter into communion with Christ and to contemplate his Face, to recognize the Lord's Face in the faces of the brethren and in daily events, we require "clean hands and a pure heart."

Clean hands, that is, a life illumined by the truth of love that overcomes indifference, doubt, falsehood and selfishness; and pure hearts are essential too, hearts enraptured by divine beauty, as the Little Teresa of Lisieux says in her prayer to the Holy Face, hearts stamped with the hallmark of the Face of Christ.

Address during a pilgrimage to the Shrine of the
Holy Face in Manoppello, Italy
September 1, 2006

64. *Metanoia*

Change of heart [is] a key point. Only in this way, in fact, is the mind freed of the limits that prevent its access to the mystery, and the eyes become capable of focusing on the face of Christ. . . . Theology can only develop in prayer that accepts God's presence and entrusts itself to him in obedience.

Message for the centenary of the birth of
Hans Urs von Balthasar
October 6, 2005

65. *Experience*

In the cities where you live and work, often chaotic and noisy, where man hurries on and loses himself, where people live as though God did not exist, may you be able to create places and opportunities for prayer, where in silence, in listening to God through *lectio divina,* in personal and communal prayer, man may encounter God and have a living experience of Jesus Christ who reveals the authentic Face of the Father.

Address to the bishops ordained during the past year
September 22, 2007

66. *Fascination*

Dear young people: let yourselves be attracted by the fascination of Christ! Fixing his Face with the eyes of the faith, ask him: "Jesus what do you want me to do with you and for you?" Thus, keep listening. Be guided by his

Spirit, second the plan he has for you. Prepare yourselves seriously and build families that are united and faithful to the Gospel and to be his witnesses in society; then, if he calls you, be ready to dedicate your whole life to his service in the Church as priests or as men and women religious. I assure you of my prayers.

Homily on the Fifth Sunday of Lent
March 29, 2009

VII. THE FACE OF CHRIST REFLECTED IN THE FACE OF THE SUFFERING AND MARGINALIZED

67. *"As you did . . . "*

In the face of every human being, and still more if tried and disfigured by sickness, shines the Face of Christ, who said: "As you did it to one of the least of these my brethren, you did it to me" (Mt 25:40).

> *Address at the 15th World Day of the Sick*
> *February 11, 2007*

68. *Care*

The faith and love we nourish for him, the Lord calls us to translate into daily gestures of care for the people we encounter, especially those experiencing moments of trial, so that in the face of each person, even more of those in need, the Face of Christ may shine forth.

> *Address to the members of the Circle of St. Peter*
> *February 22, 2008*

69. *Search*

In the modern world, which often makes beauty and physical efficiency an idea to be pursued in every possible way, we are called as Christians to discover the Face of Jesus Christ, "the fairest of the sons of men" (Ps 45[44]:2[3]), precisely in people who are suffering and marginalized.

Homily at a eucharistic concelebration in Savona
May 17, 2008

70. *Friend*

The word proclaimed and lived becomes credible if it is incarnate in behavior that demonstrates solidarity and sharing, in deeds that show the Face of Christ as man's true Friend.

Address at the pastoral convention
of the Diocese of Rome
May 26, 2009

71. *Criterion*

The Face of Christ, King of the Universe, is that of the judge, for God is at the same time a good and merciful Shepherd and a just Judge. . . . The criterion of judgment is decisive. This criterion is love, the concrete charity to neighbor, and in particular to the "little," the people in the greatest difficulties: hungry, thirsty, foreigners, naked, sick and in prison.

Address to pilgrims from the Southern Italian
Archdiocese of Amalfi-Cava De' Tirreni
November 22, 2008

72. *Vocation*

In Christ, *charity in truth* becomes the Face of his Person, a vocation for us to love our brothers and sisters in the truth of his plan. Indeed, he himself is the Truth (cf. Jn 14:6).

Encyclical Letter Caritas in Veritate (no. 1)

73. *Journey*

The . . . journey, by bringing us close to God, enables us to look upon our brethren and their needs with new eyes. Those who begin to recognize God, to look at the face of Christ, also see their brother with other eyes, discover their brother, what is good for him, what is bad for him, his needs.

General Audience
March 1, 2006

74. *Discovery*

Whoever addresses the God of Jesus Christ is spurred to serve the brethren; and vice versa, whoever dedicates himself or herself to the poor, discovers there the mysterious Face of God.

Address on the 50th anniversary of the
Charitable Works of Padre Pio of Pietrelcina
October 14, 2006

75. *With Christ*

Every person who suffers, helps Christ to carry his Cross and climbs with him the path to Golgotha in order one day to rise again with him. When we see the infamy to which Jesus was subjected, when we contemplate his face on the Cross, when we recognize his appalling suffering, we can glimpse, through faith, the radiant face of the Risen Lord who tells us that suffering and sickness will not have the last word in our human lives.

Address during a meeting with the sick
March 19, 2009

76. *Mission*

Therefore anyone who serves within the ecclesial bodies that manage charitable initiatives and structures, cannot but have this principal aim: to make the merciful Face of the Heavenly Father known and felt, for in the heart of God-Love lies the true response to the deepest expectations of every human heart.

How necessary it is for Christians to keep their gaze fixed on Christ's Face! In him alone, fully God and fully man, we may contemplate the Father (cf. Jn 14:9) and experience his infinite mercy!

Address to participants in the Plenary Assembly
of the Pontifical Council "Cor Unum"
November 13, 2009

77. *Service*

In the faces of the bereaved and dispossessed, we cannot fail to recognize the suffering face of Christ, and indeed it is he whom we serve when we show our love and compassion to those in need (cf. Mt 25:40).

Address to the bishops of Sri Lanka
May 7, 2005

VIII. THE FACE OF CHRIST REFLECTED IN THE FACE OF THE SAINTS

78. *History*

The new step is that this mysterious God liberates us from the inflation of images and from an age filled with images of divinities and gives us the freedom of vision of the essential. God appears with a face, a body, a human history, which is at the same time divine. It is a history that continues in the history of saints, martyrs, saints of charity, of the word, who are always an explanation, a continuation of his divine and human life in the Body of Christ and give us the fundamental images in which—over and above superficial images that conceal reality—we can open our gaze to Truth itself.

> *Address to the parish priests and the clergy*
> *of the Diocese of Rome*
> *February 7, 2008*

79. *Saints*

The Saints . . . in practicing the Gospel of charity, account for their hope. They show the true Face of God who is Love and, at the same time, the authentic face of man, created in the divine image and likeness.

Angelus
August 9, 2009

80. *Holy images*

In Christ we may also contemplate the Face of God and learn to be true men ourselves, true images of God. Christ invites us to imitate him, to become similar to him, so in every person the Face of God shines out anew. To tell the truth, in the Ten Commandments God forbade the making of images of God, but this was because of the temptations to idolatry to which the believer might be exposed in a context of paganism. Yet when God made himself visible in Christ through the Incarnation, it became legitimate to reproduce the Face of Christ. The holy images teach us to see God represented in the Face of Christ. After the Incarnation of the Son of God, it therefore became possible to see God in images of Christ and also in the faces of the Saints, in the faces of all people in whom God's holiness shines out.

General Audience
April 29, 2009

81. *Necessity*

Holiness is not only possible but also necessary for every person in his or her own state of life, so as to reveal to the world the true face of Christ, our friend!

> *Homily at the Holy Mass and canonization of*
> *Fr. Antônio de Sant'Ana Galvão, OFM*
> *May 11, 2007*

82. *Final exhortation*

We have talents, and our responsibility is to work so that this world may be open to Christ, that it be renewed. Yet even as we work responsibly, we realize that God is the true Judge. We are also certain that this Judge is good; we know his Face, the Face of the Risen Christ, of Christ crucified for us. Therefore we can be certain of his goodness and advance with great courage.

> *General Audience*
> *November 12, 2008*

IX. PRAYER TO THE HOLY FACE

Lord Jesus, you said to the first apostles, "What are you looking for?," and they accepted your invitation to "Come and see," recognizing you as the awaited and promised Messiah for the redemption of the world. We as well, your disciples in these difficult times, want to follow you and be your friends, drawn by the radiance of your hidden face.

We pray that you show us your face, never changing yet always new, the mysterious mirror of the infinite mercy of God. Allow us to contemplate it with the eyes of our minds and hearts: the face of the Son, splendor of the Father's glory and imprint of his substance (cf. Heb 1:3), human face of the God who entered history to unveil the horizons of eternity. The silent face of Jesus suffering and risen, who changes hearts and lives when he is loved and welcomed. "Your face, Lord, do I seek! Do not hide your face from me" (Ps 27:8-9). Over centuries and millennia, how many times has this heartrending plea of the Psalmist echoed among believers! Lord, we also echo it with faith: "Man of suffering, knowing pain, like one from who you turn your face" (Is. 53:3), do not hide your face from us! We want to draw from your eyes, so full of tenderness and compassion, the power of love and peace that may show us the path of life, and the courage to follow you without fear or compromise, to become witnesses of your Gospel with concrete actions of welcome, love, and forgiveness.

Holy Face of Christ, light that illumines the darkness of sadness and doubt, life that has defeated forever the power of evil and death, mysterious gaze that does not cease to look upon us, face concealed in the Eucharist and in the faces of those around us, make us pilgrims of God in this world, yearning for the infinite and ready for the last day when we will see you, Lord, "face to face" (1 Cor 13:12), and can contemplate you forever in the glory of Heaven.

Mary, Mother of the Holy Face, help us to have "innocent hands and pure hearts," hands illuminated by the truth of love and hearts enraptured with the divine beauty, so that, transformed by the encounter with Christ, we may give ourselves without reservation to our brothers and sisters, especially to the poor and suffering, in whose faces glows the mysterious presence of your Son Jesus, who lives and reigns forever and ever.

Amen!

INDEX

*(Numbering refers to the sequential
positioning of each thought.)*